Scripture Prayers for Everyday Use

Scripture Prayers for Everyday Use

Stephen Grunlan

Wipf & Stock
PUBLISHERS
Eugene, Oregon

Wipf and Stock Publishers
199 W 8th Ave, Suite 3
Eugene, OR 97401

Scripture Prayers for Everyday Use
By Grunlan, Stephen
Copyright©2004 by Grunlan, Stephen
ISBN: 1-59244-779-1
Publication date 8/2/2004

10   9   8   7   6   5   4   3   2   1

This book is dedicated to the people of
Grace Fellowship Church
a place where people are
transformed by God's love.

Table of Contents

Introduction

Do you ever find yourself needing to pray but not having the right words or knowing how to pray? The Bible recognizes we all find ourselves in that situation. In Romans 8:26, we read, *"We do not know what we ought to pray for…"* This passage then goes on to say the Holy Spirit will help us. I believe one of the ways the Holy Spirit helps us is through God's Word. In 2 Peter 1:20-21, we are told, *"Above all, you must understand that no prophecy of Scripture came about by the prophet's own interpretation. For prophecy never had its origin in the will of man, but men spoke from God as they were carried along by the Holy Spirit."* One of the things the Holy Spirit led the writers of Scripture to record was prayers. There are hundreds of prayers found in the Bible. I believe one of the reasons the Holy Spirit lead the writers of Scripture to record those prayers was so that they would be available for us to use. God knew there would be times we would not be able to find the right words or be able to form our prayers and so he has given us hundreds of prayers to draw on.

Now, we do not just recite these prayers by rote. Rather we make them our own. A prayer I have adopted and often use is a prayer of King Asa of Judah found in 2 Chronicles 14:11. It reads, *"Lord, there is no one like you to help the powerless against the mighty. Help us, O Lord our God, for we rely on you, and in your name we have come against this vast army. O Lord, you are our God; do not let man prevail against you."* King Asa prayed this prayer when he was facing an overwhelming Cushite army. While we do not face the Cushite army, we face problems and obstacles that seem overpowering to us and we can adopt this prayer for ourselves. For example, if I was facing a problem, I might adopt this prayer in this way: *"Lord, there is no one like you to help the powerless against these problems. Help me, O Lord my God, for I rely on you, and in your name I come against this problem* (at this point I would probably name the problem). *O Lord, you are my God, do not let this problem prevail against me."*

Some of the prayers we find in the Bible are in the plural. When we pray for ourselves we can change them to the singular. For example, another prayer I have adopted was prayed by the prophet Isaiah. It is found in Isaiah 33:2, where he prays, *"O Lord, be gracious to us, we long for you. Be our strength every morning, our salvation in time of distress."* I pray, *"O Lord, be gracious to me, I long for. Be my strength every morning, my salvation in time of distress."*

Some prayers mention Israel, the temple, Jerusalem, or some other people or place that is not relevant to us. We can still adopt the prayer by either eliminating the people or place or by changing it. For example, we find a prayer of David in Psalm 65:1-3. He prays, *"Praise awaits you, O God, in Zion; to you our vows will be fulfilled. O you who hear prayer, to you all men will come. When we were overwhelmed by sins, you forgave our transgressions."* I would pray, *"Praise awaits you, O God* (then I would eliminate *in Zion* or change it to *in my heart*); *to you my commitments will be fulfilled. O you who hear prayer, to you I come. When I am overwhelmed by sins, you forgive my transgressions."*

As I read the prayers of people in the Bible I find them saying what I want to say. I use their words to help me communicate with God. When I struggle with how to express myself to God, it helps to see how others have addressed God in similar circumstances. God has given us these prayers to aid us in our prayer lives. When Jesus disciples asked Him how to pray, He did not just say, "Say what's in your heart, use your own words." Rather, He gave them a model prayer. In the Bible we find hundreds of model prayers.

Chapter 1

Prayers of Confession and Seeking Forgiveness

What do we do when we have given in to temptation and sin? One of the greatest promises in the Bible is found in 1 John 1:9, *"If we confess our sins, [God] is faithful and just to forgive us our sins and purify us from all unrighteousness."* There is nothing God cannot forgive and will not forgive if we will confess it. One of the things about the Bible that convinces me of its truthfulness is that it presents God's people with all their faults and failures. They were constantly messing up and needing to confess their sins and ask for forgiveness. Many of their prayers of confession and seeking forgiveness are recorded for us in the Bible. Christians are not the company of the perfect but the fellowship of the forgiven.

Prayers of confession and seeking forgiveness are first because they are the key to all other prayer. The Bible tells us in Isaiah 59:1-2, *Surely the arm of the Lord is not too short to save, not his ear too dull to hear. But your iniquities have separated you from your God; your sins have hidden his face from you, so that he will not hear.* Unconfessed sin blocks our prayer because it interferes with our communion with God. The good news, as we have already seen, is that God is waiting for us to come in confession so he can forgive us. These prayers were recorded in Scripture for us so we would know how to pray when we have sinned and need to confess and seek forgiveness.

I have sinned greatly by doing this. Now I beg you, take away the guilt of your servant. I have done a very foolish thing. 1 Chronicles 21:8

O, my God, I am too ashamed and disgraced to lift my face to you, my God, because our sins are higher than our heads and our guilt has reached to the heavens...now, O our God, what can we say after this? For we have disregarded the commands you gave..." Ezra 9:6,10,11

O Lord, God of heaven, the great and awesome God, who keeps his covenant of love with those who love him and obey his commands, let your ear be attentive and your eyes open to hear the prayer your servant is praying before you day and night…I confess the sins we Israelites, including myself and my father's house, have committed against you. We have acted very wickedly toward you. We have not obeyed your commands…" Nehemiah 1:5-7

Who can discern his errors? Forgive my hidden faults. Keep your servant also from willful sins; may they not rule over me. Then will I be blameless and innocent of great transgression. Psalm 19:12-13

Remember, O Lord, your great mercy and love, for they are from old. Remember not the sins of my youth and my rebellious ways; according to your love remember me, for you are good, O Lord. Psalm 25:6-7

O Lord, do not rebuke me in your anger or discipline me in your wrath…My guilt has overwhelmed me like a burden too heavy to bear…because of my sinful folly I am bowed down and brought very low…I wait for you, O Lord; you will answer me, O my God…I confess my iniquity, I am troubled by my sin…O Lord, do not forsake me; be not far from me, O my God. Come quickly to help me, O lord my Savior. Psalm 38:1,4,5,6,15,18,21,22

Do not withhold your mercy from me, O Lord; may your love and truth always protect me…my sins have overtaken me, and I cannot see. They are more than the hairs of my head, and my heart fails within me. Be pleased, O Lord to save me; O Lord, come quickly to help me. Psalm 40:11-13

O Lord, have mercy on me; heal me, for I have sinned against you. Psalm 41:4

Have mercy on me, O God, according to you unfailing love; according to your great compassion blot out my transgressions. Wash away all *my iniquity and cleanse me from my sin. For I know my transgressions, and my sin is always before me. Against you, you only, have I sinned and done what is evil in your sight, so you are proved right when you speak and justified when you judge. Surely I was sinful at birth, sinful from the time my mother conceived me. Surely you desire truth in the inner parts; you teach me wisdom in the inmost place. Cleanse me with hyssop, and I will be clean; wash me, and I will be whiter than snow. Let me hear joy and gladness; let the bones you have crushed rejoice. Hide your face from my sins and blot out my iniquity. Create in me a pure heart, O God, and renew a steadfast spirit within me.* Psalm 51:1-10*

You know my folly, O God; my guilt is not hidden from you. May those who hope in you not be disgraced because of me, O Lord, the Lord Almighty; may those who seek you not be put to shame because of me, O God…But I pray to you, O Lord, in the time of your favor; in your great love, O God, answer me with your sure salvation. Answer me, O Lord, out of the goodness of your love; in your great mercy turn to me. Psalm 69:5,6,13,16

May your mercy come quickly to meet us, for we are in desperate need. Help us, O God our Savior, for the glory of your name; deliver us and forgive our sins for your name's sake. Psalm 79:8-9

You showed favor to your land, O Lord…You forgave the iniquity of your people and covered all their sins. You set aside all your wrath and turn from your fierce anger. Restore us again, O God our Savior, and put away your displeasure toward us…Show us your unfailing love, O Lord. Psalm 85:1-4,6

You are forgiving and good, O Lord, abounding in love to all who call on you. Hear my prayer, O Lord; listen to my cry for mercy…you are a compassionate and gracious God, slow to anger, abounding in love and faithfulness. Turn to me and have mercy on me. Psalm 86:5-6,15-16

O Lord, hear my voice, let you ears be attentive to my cry for mercy. If you, O Lord, kept a record of sins, O Lord who could stand? But with you there is forgiveness; therefore you are feared. Psalm 130:2-4

Search me, O God, and know my heart; test me and know my anxious thoughts. See if there is any offensive way in me, and lead me in the way everlasting. Psalm 139:23-24

O Lord, we acknowledge our wickedness and guilt…we have sinned against you. For the sake of your name do not despise us… O Lord our God…our hope is in you. Jeremiah 14:20,21,22

O Lord, the great and awesome God, who keeps his covenant of love with all who love him and obey his commands, we have sinned and done wrong. We have been wicked and rebelled; we have turned away from your commands and laws…We do not make requests of you because we are righteous, but because of your great mercy. O Lord, listen! O Lord forgive! Daniel 9:4-5,18-19

Who is a God like you, who pardons sin and forgives…? You do not stay angry forever but delight to show mercy. You will again have compassion on us; you will tread our sins underfoot and hurl all our iniquities into the depths of the sea. Micah 7:18-19

Forgive us our debts, as we also have forgiven our debtors. Matthew 6:12

Chapter 2

Prayers for Dealing with Temptation and Sin

Have you seen the bumper sticker that reads, "Lead me not into temptation, I can find it myself"? The reality is, whether we are led into temptation or find it ourselves, temptation is part of life. We live in a society that offers temptations previous generations could not even imagine. We also live in a permissive society where the social restraints that helped people resist temptation in the past are no longer in place. While we may face more temptations and have less social restraints than at any time in human history, temptation and sin have been part of the human experience since the Garden of Eden. People in the Bible were subject to temptation and sin and recognized their vulnerability, so they turned to God for help. God's help is also available to us. The prayers of those people in the Bible are available to us as we struggle with temptation and sin.

Though you probe my heart and examine me at night, though you test me, you will find nothing; I have resolved that my mouth will not sin. As for the deeds of men—by the word of your lips I have kept myself from the ways of the violent. My steps have held to your paths; my feet have not slipped. Psalm 17:3-5

Keep your servant also from willful sins; may they not rule over me. Then I will be blameless, innocent of great transgression. May the words of my mouth and the meditation of my heart be pleasing in your sight, O Lord my Rock and Redeemer. Psalm 19:13-14

Test me, O Lord, and try me, examine my heart and mind; for your love is ever before me, and I walk continually in your truth. Psalm 26:2-3

I will sing of your love and justice; to you, O Lord I will sing praise. I will be careful to lead a blameless life…I will walk in my house with blameless heart. I set before my eyes no vile thing. The deeds of faithless men I hate; they will not cling to me. Men of perverse heart shall be far from me; I will have nothing to do with evil. Psalm 101:1-4 (for the negative effect of ungodly people on us see Proverbs 13:20 and 1 Corinthians 15:33-34)

I seek you with all my heart; do not let me stray from your commands. I have hidden your word in my heart that I might not sin against you. Praise be to you, O Lord, teach me your decrees. Psalm 119:10-12

Direct my footsteps according to your word; let no sin rule over me. Psalm 119:133

Set a guard over my mouth, O Lord; keep watch over the door of my lips. Let not my heart be drawn to what is evil, to take part in wicked deeds. Psalm 141:3-4

I know, O Lord, that a man's life is not his own; it is not for man to direct his steps. Correct me, O Lord, but with justice – not in your anger. Jeremiah 10:23-24

Lead us not into temptation but deliver us from the evil one. Matthew 6:18

Chapter 3

Prayers for Guidance and Wisdom

As believers we want to do God's will. However, to follow his will, we need to know his will. While much of God's will for us is revealed directly in the Bible, there are times when his will in a specific situation is not found in his Word. At those times we need to turn to him for guidance. In the Bible, people who wanted to follow God's direction turned to him in prayer and asked for guidance. Those prayers are available to us as we seek guidance for our lives.

In the Bible, wisdom has nothing to do with intelligence or education. Rather, wisdom is knowing God's will and knowing how to carry it out. That is why the Bible says over and over, *"The fear of the Lord is the beginning of wisdom"* (Psalm 111:10; Proverbs 1:7; 9:10; 15:33; ; Micah 6:9). The Bible tells us in James 1:5, *"If any of you lacks wisdom, he should ask God, who gives generously to all without finding fault, and it will be given to him."* Throughout the Bible we find people asking God for wisdom. Their prayers are available to us as we ask God for wisdom. For example, we can adopt the prayers of Solomon for wisdom to lead Israel when we have been given a task that is beyond our wisdom, such as parenting, leading a Bible study or a ministry team, or taking on a position of leadership in the church.

If you are pleased with me, teach me your ways so that I may know you and continue to find favor with you. Exodus 33:13

So give your servant a discerning heart to govern your people and to distinguish between right and wrong. For who is able to govern this great people of yours? 1 Kings 3:9

Give me wisdom and knowledge, that I may lead this people, for who is able to govern this great people of yours? 2 Chronicles 1:10

O our God...we have no power to face this vast army attacking us. We do not know what to do, but our eyes are upon you. 2 Chronicles 20:12

But I, by your great mercy, will come into your house; in reverence I will bow down... Lead me, O Lord, in your righteousness. Psalm 5:7-8

Show me your ways, O Lord, teach me your paths; guide me in your truth and teach me, for you are God my Savior, and my hope is in you all day long. Psalm 25:4-5

Teach me your way, O Lord; lead me in a straight path. Psalm 27:11

Send forth your light and your truth, let them guide me. Psalm 43:4

Teach me your way, O Lord, and I will walk in your truth; give me an undivided heart, that I may fear your name. Psalm 86:11

Teach me, O Lord, to follow your decrees; then I will keep them to the end. Give me understanding, and I will keep your law and obey it with all my heart. Direct me in the path of your commands, for there I find delight. Psalm 119:33-35

Do good to your servant according to your Word, O lord. Teach me knowledge and good judgment for I believe in your commands. Psalm 119:65-66

Deal with your servant according to your love and teach me your decrees. I am your servant; give me discernment that I may understand your statutes... Direct my footsteps according to your Word, let no sin rule over me. Psalm 119:125,133

I keep asking that the God of our Lord Jesus Christ, the glorious Father, may give you the Spirit of wisdom and revelation, so that you may know him better. I pray also that the eyes of your heart may be enlightened in order that you may know the hope to which he has called you, the riches of his glorious inheritance in the saints, and his incomparably great power for us who believe. Ephesians 1:17-19

We have not stopped praying for you and asking God to fill you with the knowledge of his will through all spiritual wisdom and understanding. Colossians 1:9

Chapter 4

Prayers for Help

Where do we turn when we need help? If we are honest, we have to admit it is often everywhere but to the Lord. We turn to friends and family, we turn to accountants and lawyers, we turn to counselors and doctors, we turn to human sources of help. Now, God often uses human means to help us. However, we need to turn to him first. We are not the only ones who need God's help. In the Bible many of God's children needed his help and turned to him for help. God heard their prayers and came to their aid. The truth is, God delights in helping His children. He encourages us to come to him for help in time of trouble. Sometimes we do not know what or how to pray. At those times we can look to the prayers for help uttered by people in the Bible. They were recorded for us to use in our times of trouble.

O Lord God...enthroned between the cherubim, you alone are God over all the kingdoms of the earth. You have made heaven and earth. Give ear, O Lord, and hear; open your eyes, O Lord and see... Now, O Lord, delivers us...for you alone are God. 2 Kings 19:15,16,19

O that you would bless me and enlarge my territory! Let your hand be with me, and keep me from harm so that I will be free from pain. 1 Chronicles 4:10

Lord, there is no one like you to help the powerless against the mighty. Help us, O Lord our God, for we rely on you, and in your name we have come against this vast army. O Lord, you are our God; do not let man prevail against you. 2 Chronicles 14:11

O Lord, God of heaven, the great and awesome God, who keeps his covenant of love with those who love him and obey his commands, let your ear be attentive and your eyes open to hear the prayer your servant is praying before you night and day… O, Lord, let your ear be attentive to the prayer of this your servant…give your servant success. Nehemiah 1:5-6,11

Answer me when I call to you, O my righteous God. Give me relief from my distress; be merciful to me and hear my prayer. Psalm 4:1

How long, O Lord? Will you forget me forever? How long will you hide your face from me? How long must I wrestle with my thoughts and every day have sorrow in my heart? …Look on me and answer, O Lord my God…I trust in your unfailing love; my heart rejoices in your salvation. Psalm 13:1-3,5

To you I call, O Lord my Rock; do not turn a deaf ear to me. For if you remain silent I will be like those who have gone down to the pit. Hear my cry for mercy as I call for your help, as I lift up my hands toward your most holy place. Psalm 28:1-2

O Lord, do not forsake me; be not far from me, O my God… Come quickly to help me, O Lord my Savior. Psalm 38:21-22

Hear my prayer, O Lord, listen to my cry for help, be not deaf to my weeping. Psalm 39:12

Do not withhold your mercy from me, O Lord; may your love and your truth always protect me… Be pleased, O Lord, to save me; O Lord come quickly to help me… You are my help and my deliverer; O my God, do not delay. Psalm 40:11,13,17

Save me, O God, by your name; vindicate me by your might. Hear my prayer, O God; listen to the words of my mouth. Psalm 54:1-2

Listen to my prayer, O God, do not ignore my plea; hear me and answer me. My thoughts trouble me and I am distraught. Psalm 55:1-2

Hear my cry, O Lord, listen to my prayer. From the ends of the earth

I call to you. I call as my heart grows faint; lead me to the rock that is higher than I. For you have been my refuge and a strong tower against the foe. I long to dwell in your tent forever and take refuge in the shelter of your wings. Psalm 61:1-4

Save me, O God, for the waters have come up to my neck. I sink in the miry depths, where there is no foothold... I have come into the deep waters; the floods engulf me. I am worn out calling for help; my throat is parched... I pray to you, O Lord, in the time of your favor; in your great love, O God, answer me with your sure salvation... Answer me, O Lord, out of the goodness of your love; in your great mercy turn to me. Psalm 69:1-3,13,16

In you, O Lord, I have taken refuge; let me not be put to shame. Rescue me and deliver me in your righteousness; turn your ear and save me. Be my rock of refuge to which I can always go; give the command to save me, for you are my rock and my fortress... Be not far from me, O God; come quickly, O my God to help me... But as for me I will always have hope; I will praise you more and more. My mouth will tell of your righteousness, of your salvation all day long. Psalm 71:1-3,12,14,15

May your mercy come quickly to meet us, for we are in desperate need. Help us, O God our Savior, for the glory of your name; deliver us and forgive our sins for your name's sake. Psalm 79:8-9

Hear, O Lord, and answer me for I am poor and needy. Guard my life for I am devoted to you. You are my God, save your servant who trusts in you. Have mercy on me, O Lord, for I call to you all day long... Hear my prayer, O Lord; listen to my cry for mercy. In the day of my trouble I will call to you for you will answer me... Turn to me and have mercy on me; grant your strength to your servant. Psalm 86:1-3,6,7,16

O Lord, the God who saves me, day and night I cry out before you. Do not hide your face from me when I am in distress. Turn your ear to me when I call, answer me quickly. Psalm 102:1-2

O Sovereign Lord, deal well with me for your name's sake; out of the goodness of your love deliver me… Help me. O Lord my God; save me in accordance with your love. Psalm 109:21,26

I will call with all my heart; answer me, O Lord, and I will obey your decrees. I call out to you, save me and I will keep your statutes. I rise before dawn and cry for help, I have put my hope in your word. My eyes stay open through the watches of the night, that I may meditate on your promises. Hear my voice in accordance with your love. Psalm 119:145-149

O Lord, be gracious to us; we long for you. Be our strength every morning, our salvation in time of distress. Isaiah 33:2

I called on your name, O Lord, from the depths of the pit. You heard my plea; do not close your ear to my cry for relief. Lamentations 3:58

Now our God, hear the prayers and petitions of your servant. For your sake, O Lord, look with favor on your desolate sanctuary. Give ear, O God and hear; open your eyes and see the desolation of the city that bears your Name. We do not make requests of you because we are righteous, but because of your great mercy. O Lord, listen. O Lord, Forgive! O Lord, hear and act! For your sake, O my God, do not delay, because your city and your people bear your name. Daniel 9:17-19 (This is a prayer that could be modified and used for a church)

How long, O Lord, must I call for help; but you do not listen? Or cry out to you, but you do not save? …O Lord, are you not from everlasting? My God, my Holy One, we will not die. Habakkuk 1:2,12

Chapter 5

Prayers for Insight into God's Will and Word

Believers down through the ages have wanted to have insight into God's will and God's Word. The incredible thing is, God wants us to understand his Word and his will for us more than we do. God loves us and his commands are for our guidance and protection. They were given so we could become all he created us to be. God is not out to limit us or restrict us. God is not out to deny us or keep us from enjoying life. Just the opposite, he wants us to get the most out of life. When we choose to ignore him and his Word and go our own way we end up hurting and limiting ourselves. When we go God's way we benefit and are free to become all we can be. This is why it is so important for us to have insight into God's Word and his will for us. The people in the Bible understood this and asked for this insight. We can use their prayers to ask God to give us insight into his Word and His Will.

Open my eyes that I may see wonderful things in your law. I am a stranger on earth; do not hide your commands from me... Let me understand the teaching of your precepts; then I will meditate on your wonders. Psalm 119:18,19,26

Teach me, O Lord, to follow your decrees; then I will keep them to the end. Give me understanding and I will keep your law and obey it with all my heart. Direct me in the path of your commands, for there I find delight... Your hands formed me and made me; give me understanding to learn your commands. Psalm 119:65,66,73

Deal with your servant according to your love and teach me your decrees. I am your servant; give me discernment that I may understand your statutes. Psalm 119:124-125

May my cry come before you, O Lord; give me understanding according to your word. Psalm 119:169

I keep asking that the God of our Lord Jesus Christ, the glorious Father, may give you the Spirit of wisdom and revelation, so that you may know him better. I pray also that the eyes of your heart may be enlightened in order that you may know the hope to which he has called you, the riches of his glorious inheritance in the saints, and his incomparably great power for us who believe. Ephesians 1:17-19

For this reason I kneel before the Father, from whom his whole family in heaven and on earth derives its name. I pray that out of his glorious riches he may strengthen you with power through his Spirit in your inner being, so that Christ may dwell in your hearts through faith. And I pray that you, being rooted and established in love, may have power, together with all the saints, to grasp how wide and deep is the love of Christ and to know this love that surpasses knowledge – that you may be filled to the measure of all the fullness of God. Ephesians 3:14-19

And this is our prayer: that your love may abound more and more in knowledge and depth of insight, so that you may be able to discern what is best and may be pure and blameless until the day of Christ, filled with the fruit of righteousness that comes through Christ Jesus— to the glory and praise of God. Philippians 1:9-11

Chapter 6

Prayers for Mercy

Justice is an important value in our society, but the reality is most of us do not want justice for ourselves, we want mercy. If we are stopped by a police officer when we were going over the speed limit, we do not want justice, which would be to get a ticket. Rather, we want mercy, we want the police officer to let us off with a warning. The same is true with God. We do not want justice, we do not want to receive what we deserve, we want mercy. Fortunately we have a merciful God we can turn to. We are not alone in our need for mercy. Since sin entered the world everyone has stood in need of mercy. It is not surprising to find a number of prayers for mercy in the Bible. They are there for us to use.

Give attention to your servant's prayer and his plea for mercy, O Lord my God. Hear the cry and the prayer that your servant is praying in your presence. 2 Chronicles 6:19

Answer me when I call to you, O my righteous God. Give me relief from my distress; be merciful to me and hear my prayer. Psalm 4:1

O Lord, do not rebuke me in your anger or discipline me in your wrath. Be merciful to me, O Lord... " Psalm 6:1-2

Hear my voice when I call, O Lord; be merciful to me and answer me. My heart says of you, "Seek his face!" Your face, Lord, I seek. Do not hide your face from me, do not turn your servant away in anger; you have been my helper... Teach me your way, O Lord; lead me in a straight path. Psalm 27:7-9,11

To you I call, O lord my Rock; do not turn a deaf ear to me... Hear my cry for mercy as I call to you for help... Psalm 28:1-2

Hear, O Lord, and be merciful to me; O Lord, be my help. You turned my wailing into dancing; you removed my sackcloth and clothed me with joy, that my heart may sing to you and not be silent. O Lord, my God, I will give you thanks forever. Psalm 30:10-12

To you I call, O Lord my Rock; do not turn a deaf ear to me. For if you remain silent I will be like those who have gone down to the pit. Hear my cry for mercy as I call for your help, as I lift up my hands toward your most holy place. Psalm 28:1-2

Be merciful to me, O Lord, for I am in distress; my eyes grow weak with sorrow, my soul and my body with grief… But I trust in you, "O Lord; I say, "You are my God." My times are in your hands… Psalm 31:9,10,14,15

Do not withhold your mercy from me, O Lord; may your love and your truth always protect me… Be pleased, O Lord, to save me; O Lord come quickly to help me… You are my help and my deliverer; O my God, do not delay. Psalm 40:11,13,17

O Lord have mercy on me; heal me for I have sinned against you. Psalm 41:4

Be merciful to me, O God… When I am afraid, I will trust in you. In God whose word I praise, in God I trust; I will not be afraid. Psalm 56:1,3

Have mercy on me, O God, have mercy on me, for in you my soul takes refuge. I will take refuge in the shadow of your wing until the disaster has passed. Psalm 57:1

I pray to you, O Lord, in the time of your favor; in your great love, O God, answer me with your sure salvation… Answer me, O Lord, out of the goodness of your love; in your great mercy turn to me. Psalm 69:13,16

May your mercy come quickly to meet us, for we are in desperate need. Help us, O God our Savior, for the glory of your name; deliver us and forgive our sins for your name's sake. Psalm 79:8-9

Hear, O Lord and answer me, for I am poor and needy. Guard my life, for I am devoted to you. You are my God, save your servant who trusts in you. Have mercy on me, O Lord, for I call to you all day long. Bring joy to your servant, for to you, O Lord, I lift up my soul. You are forgiving and good, O Lord, abounding in love to all who call to you. Hear my prayer, O Lord, listen to my cry for mercy. In the day of my trouble I will call to you, for you will answer me. Psalm 86:1-7

You, O Lord, are a compassionate and gracious God, slow to anger, abounding in love and faithfulness. Turn to me and have mercy on me; grant your strength to your servant. Psalm 86:15-16

Turn to me and have mercy on me, as you always do to those who love your name. Psalm 119:132

I lift up my eyes to you, to you whose throne is in heaven… Have mercy on us, O Lord, have mercy on us. Psalm 123:1,3

Out of the depths I cry to you, O Lord; O Lord hear my voice. Let your ears be attentive to my cry for mercy. Psalm 130:1-2

You are my God, hear, O Lord, my cry for mercy. O Sovereign Lord, my strong deliverer who shields my head… Psalm 140:6-7

O Lord, hear my prayer, listen to my cry for mercy; in your faithfulness and righteousness come to my relief. Psalm 143:1

Lord, I have heard of your fame; I stand in awe of your deeds, O Lord renew them in our day, in our time make them known; in wrath remember mercy. Habbakuk 3:2

Chapter 7

Prayers of Praise

What is the difference between praise and worship? While praise and worship do overlap and are sometimes used interchangeably, there is a general distinction. Praise is generally used to recognize and give honor to God for the things He does. We praise God for His acts of love, mercy and grace. Worship is recognizing who God is, His character and attributes. God is worthy of our praise and worship. If we are really honest, many of us would have to admit we find it easier to pray for others and ourselves than to offer God praise and worship. Part of the reason for that is we know how to ask for things but we are not always sure how to offer praise and worship. Yet the Bible commands us to praise and worship God. The Bible also gives us many prayers of praise and worship we can use directly or adapt for our use. In a later chapter we will see some prayers of worship, here we have some prayers of praise.

Praise for Answered Prayer

Praise awaits you, O God... O you who hear prayer, to you all men will come... You answer us with awesome deeds of righteousness, O God our Savior, the hope of all the ends of the earth and of the farthest seas. Psalm 65:1,2,5

I will give thanks, for you answered me; you have become my salvation... You are my God, and I will give you thanks; you are my God, and I will exalt you. Psalm 118:21,28

I will praise you, O Lord, with all my heart... I will bow down toward your holy temple and will praise your name for your love and faithfulness, for you have exalted above all things your name and your word. When I called, you answered me; you made me bold and stouthearted. Psalm 138:1-3

Praise be to the name of God forever and ever; wisdom and power are his. He changes times and seasons. He sets up kings and deposes them. He gives wisdom to the wise and knowledge to the discerning. He reveals deep and hidden things, he knows what lies in darkness, and light dwells in him. I thank and praise you, O God of my fathers; you have given me wisdom and power, you made known to me what we asked of you. Daniel 2:20-23

Praise for Creation

Blessed be your glorious name, and may it be exalted above all blessing and praise. You alone are the Lord. You made the heavens, even the highest heavens, and all their starry host, the earth and all that is on it, the seas and all that is in them. You give life to everything and the multitudes of heaven worship you. Nehemiah 9:5-6

O Lord, our Lord, how majestic is your name in all the earth! You have set your glory above the heaven. From the lips of children and infants you have ordained praise… When I consider your heavens, the work of your fingers, the moon and the stars, which you have set in place, what is man that you are mindful of him, the son of man that you care for him? You made him a little lower than the heavenly beings and crowned him with glory and honor. You made him ruler over the works of your hands; you put everything under his feet; all flocks and herds, and beasts of the field, the birds of the air, and the fish of the sea, all that swims the paths of the sea. O Lord, our Lord, how majestic is your name in all the earth. Psalm 8:1-9

Praise awaits you, O God… O God our Savior, the hope of the ends of all the earth and of the farthest seas, who formed the mountains by your power, having armed yourself with strength, who stilled the roaring seas, the roaring of their waves, and the turmoil of the nations. Those living far away fear your wonders; where morning dawns and evening fades you call forth songs of joy. You care for the land and water it; you enrich it abundantly. The streams of God are filled with water to provide the people with grain, for so you have ordained it. You drench its furrows and level its ridges; you soften it with showers and bless its crops. You crown the year with your bounty, and your carts overflow with abundance. The grasslands of the desert overflow; the hills are clothed with gladness. The meadows are covered with flocks and the valleys are mantled with grain; they shout for joy and sing. Psalm 65:1,5-13

Lord you have been our dwelling place throughout all generations. Before the mountains were born or you brought forth the earth and the world, from everlasting to everlasting. Psalm 90:1-2

O Lord, you have searched me and you know me... You created my inmost being; you knit me together in my mother's womb. I praise you because I am fearfully and wonderfully made; your works are wonderful, I know that full well. My frame was not hidden from you when I was made in the secret place. When I was woven together in the depths of the earth, your eyes saw my unformed body. All the days ordained for me were written in your book before one of them came to be. Psalm 139:1,13-16

Ah Sovereign Lord, you have made the heavens and the earth by your great power and outstretched arm. Nothing is to hard for you. You show love to thousands...O Great and powerful God, whose name is Lord Almighty, great are your purposes and mighty are your deeds. Jeremiah 32:17-19

You are worthy, Our Lord and God, to receive glory and honor and power, for you created all things, and by your will they were created and have their being. Revelation 4:11

Praise for Forgiveness

Blessed be your glorious name, and may it be exalted above all blessing and praise...you are a forgiving God, gracious and compassionate, slow to anger and abounding in love. Nehemiah 9:5,17

Praise awaits you, O God...O you who hear prayer, to you all men will come. When we were overwhelmed by our sins, you forgave our transgressions. Blessed are those you choose and bring near to live in your courts. Psalm 65:1-4

If you, O Lord, kept a record of sins, O Lord who could stand? But with you there is forgiveness; therefore you are feared. Psalm 130:3-4

Praise for Grace

Blessed be your glorious name, and may it be exalted above all blessing and praise...you are a forgiving God, gracious and compassionate, slow to anger and abounding in love. Nehemiah 9:5,17

You, O Lord, are a compassionate and gracious God, slow to anger and abounding in love and faithfulness. Psalm 86:15

Praise for Greatness

Praise to you, O Lord, God of our father Israel, from everlasting to everlasting. Yours, O Lord, is the greatness and the power and the glory and the majesty and the splendor. For everything in heaven and earth is yours. Yours, O Lord is the kingdom; you are exalted as head over all. 1 Chronicles 29:10-11

Lord you have been our dwelling place throughout all generations. Before the mountains were born or you brought forth the earth and the world, from everlasting to everlasting. Psalm 90:1-2

It is good to praise the Lord and make music to your name, O Most High, to proclaim your love in the morning and your faithfulness at night...for you make me glad by your deeds, O Lord; I sing for joy at the works of your hands. How great are your works, O Lord, how profound are your thoughts... You, O Lord, are exalted forever. Psalm 92:1,2,4,5,8

I will exalt you, my God, the King; I will praise your name forever and ever. Every day I will praise you and extol your name forever and ever. Great is the Lord and most worthy of praise, his greatness no one can fathom. Psalm 145:1-3

Praise for Help

You are my lamp, O Lord; the Lord turns my darkness into light. With your help I can advance against a troop; with God I can scale a wall. 2 Samuel 22:29-30

I will praise you as long as I live, and in your name I will lift up my hands… On my bed I remember you; I think of you through the watches of the night. Because you are my help, I sing in the shadow of your wings. My soul clings to you; your right hand upholds me. Psalm 63:4,6-8

I am always with you; you hold me by your right hand. You guide me with your counsel, and afterward you will take me into glory. Whom have I in heaven but you. And earth has nothing I desire besides you. My flesh and my heart may fail, but God is the strength of my heart and my portion forever. Psalm 73:23-26

Blessed be your glorious name, and may it be exalted above all blessing and praise…you are a forgiving God, gracious and compassionate, slow to anger and abounding in love. Nehemiah 9:5,17

Praise for Love

Who among the Gods is like you, O Lord? Who is like you in majestic holiness, awesome in glory, working wonders? …In your unfailing love you will lead the people you have redeemed. Exodus 15:11,13

Blessed be your glorious name, and may it be exalted above all blessing and praise… You are a forgiving, gracious and compassionate God, slow to anger and abounding in love. Nehemiah 9:5,17

Your love, O Lord, reaches to the heavens, your faithfulness to the skies. Your righteousness is like the mighty mountains, your justice like the great deep... How priceless is your unfailing love... For with you is the fountain of life; in your light we see light. Continue your love to those who know you, your righteousness to the upright in heart. Psalm 36:5,6,7,9,10

Be exalted, O God, above all the heavens; let your glory be over all the earth... I will praise you, O Lord, among the nations; I will sing of you among the peoples. For great is your love, reaching to the heavens; your faithfulness reaches to the skies. Be exalted, O God above all the heavens; let your glory be over all the earth. Psalm 57:5,9-11

O God, you are my God, earnestly I seek you; my soul thirsts for you, my body longs for you, in a dry and weary land where there is no water... Because your love is better than life, my lips will glorify you. I will praise you as long as I live, and in your name I will lift up my hands. Psalm 63:1,3,4

I will praise you, O Lord my God, with all my heart; I will glorify your name forever; for great is your love toward me. Psalm 86:12-13

I will sing of the Lord's great love forever; with my mouth I will make your faithfulness known through all generations. I will declare that your love stands firm forever, that you established your faithfulness in heaven itself. Psalm 89:1-2

It is good to praise the Lord and make music to your name, O Most High, to proclaim your love in the morning and your faithfulness at night...you, O Lord, are exalted forever. Psalm 92:1,2,8

Not to us, O Lord, not to us, but to your name be glory because of your love and faithfulness. Psalm 115:1

Praise for Power

Praise be to you, O Lord… Yours, O Lord is the greatness and the power and the glory and the majesty and the splendor, for everything in heaven and earth is yours. Yours, O Lord is the kingdom; you are exalted as head over all. Wealth and honor come from you; you are the ruler of all things. In your hands are strength and power to exalt and to give strength to all. Now, our God, we give you thanks and praise your glorious name. 1 Chronicles 29:10-13

O God, you are my God, earnestly I seek you; my soul thirsts for you, my body longs for you, in a dry and weary land where there is no water. I have seen you in the sanctuary and beheld you power and your glory…my lips will glorify you. Psalm 63:1-3

Your ways, O God, are holy. What god is so great as our God? You are the God who performs miracles; you display your power among the peoples. Psalm 77:13-14

The heavens praise your wonders, O Lord, your faithfulness too, in the assembly of the holy ones… O Lord God Almighty, who is like you? You are mighty, O Lord, and your faithfulness surrounds you… Your arm is endued with power; your hand is strong, your right hand exalted. Righteousness and justice are the foundation of your throne; love and faithfulness go before you. Blessed are those who learn to acclaim you, who walk in the light of your presence, O Lord. Psalm 89:5,8,12-15

Ah Sovereign Lord, you have made the heavens and the earth by your great power and outstretched arm. Nothing is to hard for you. You show love to thousands…O Great and powerful God, whose name is Lord Almighty, great are your purposes and mighty are your deeds. Jeremiah 32:17-19

Praise be to the name of God forever and ever; wisdom and power are his. Daniel 2:20

We give thanks to you, Lord God Almighty, the One who is and who was, because you have taken your great power and begun to reign. Revelation 11:17

Praise for Protection

I love you, O Lord my strength... I call to the Lord who is worthy of praise... You save the humble... You, O Lord, keep my lamp burning; my God turns my darkness into light. With you help I can advance against a troop; with my God I can scale a wall. As for God his way is perfect; the word of the Lord is flawless. He is a shield for all who take refuge in him. Psalm 18:1,3,27-30

You are my hiding place; you will protect me from trouble and surround me with songs of deliverance. Psalm 32:7

I will sing of your strength, in the morning I will sing of your love; for you are my fortress, my refuge in times of trouble. O my strength. I sing praise to you; you, O God, are my fortress, my loving God. Psalm 59:16-17

I will praise you as long as I live, and in your name I will lift up my hands... On my bed I remember you; I think of you through the watches of the night. Because you are my help, I sing in the shadow of your wings. My soul clings to you; your right hand upholds me. Psalm 63:4,6-8

Though I walk in the midst of trouble, you preserve my life; you stretch out your hand against the anger of my foes, with your right hand you save me. Psalm 138:7

O Lord, you are my God; I will exalt you and praise your name, for in perfect faithfulness you have done marvelous things... You have been a refuge for the poor, a refuge for the needy in his distress, a shelter from the storm and a shade from the heat. Isaiah 25:1,4

O Lord, my strength and my fortress, my refuge in time of distress, to you the peoples will come. Jeremiah 16:19

Praise for Salvation

I trust in your unfailing love; my heart rejoices in your salvation. Psalm 13:5

My mouth will tell of your righteousness, of your salvation all day long, though I know not its measure. I will come and proclaim your mighty acts, O Sovereign Lord; I will proclaim your righteousness, yours alone... My lips will shout for joy when I sing praise to you, I whom you have redeemed. My tongue will tell of your righteous acts all day long... Psalm 71:15,16,23,24

You are the God who performs miracles; you display your power among the peoples. With your mighty arm you redeemed your people... Psalm 77:13-15

You are worthy...because you were slain, and with your blood you purchased men for God from every tribe and language and people and nation. You made them to be a kingdom and priests to serve our God... Worthy is the Lamb who was slain to receive power and wealth and wisdom and strength and honor and glory and praise. Revelation 5:9,10,12

Praise for Works

I will praise you, O Lord, with all my heart; I will tell of all your wonders. I will be glad and rejoice in you; I will sing praise to your name, O Most High. Psalm 9:1-2

I will praise you forever for what you have done; in your name I will hope for your name is good. I will praise you in the presence of your saints. Psalm 52:9

Your righteousness reaches to the skies, O God, you who have done great things. Who, O God, is like you? ...My lips will shout for joy when I sing praise to you, I whom you have redeemed. My tongue will tell of your righteous acts all day long... Psalm 71:19,23,24

I will remember your miracles of long ago. I will meditate on all your works and consider all your mighty deeds. Your ways, O God, are holy. What god is so great as our God? You are the God who performs miracles; you display your power among the peoples. With your mighty arm you redeemed your people... Psalm 77:12-15

How great are your works, O Lord, how profound your thoughts! You...O Lord are exalted forever. Psalm 92:5,9

O Lord, you are my God; I will exalt you and praise your name, for in perfect faithfulness you have done marvelous things... Isaiah 25:1

Lord, I have heard of your fame; I stand in awe of your deeds, O Lord renew them in our day, in our time make them known; in wrath remember mercy. Habbakuk 3:2

Great and marvelous are your deeds, Lord God Almighty. Just and true are your ways, O King of the Ages. Who will not fear you, O Lord, and bring glory to your name? For you alone are holy. All nations will come and worship before you, your righteous acts have been revealed. Revelation 15:3-4

Praise for God's Word

I will praise you with an upright heart as I learn your righteous laws. I will obey your decrees... Your word, O Lord, is eternal; it stands firm in the heavens. Your faithfulness continues through all generations; you established the earth and it endures. Your laws endure to this day for all things serve you... O how I love your law! I meditate on it all day long... How sweet are your words to my taste, sweeter than honey to my mouth... Your word is a lamp to my feet and a light to my path... Your statutes are my heritage forever; they are the joy of my heart. My heart is set on keeping your decrees to the very end. Psalm 119:7,8,89-91,97,103,105,111,112

When your words came, I ate them; they were my joy and my heart's delight, for I bear your name, O Lord God Almighty. Jeremiah 15:16

Chapter 8

Prayers for Protection

In a world ruled by Satan (John 12:31; 2 Corinthians 4:4) and contaminated by sin we are weak and vulnerable. Where do we turn for protection? The same place the saints in the Bible turned, to God. The Bible tells us that God will protect those who trust in Him (Psalm 32:7; 41:2; 2 Thessalonians 3:3). Here are the prayers people in the Bible used to call on God for protection.

O that you would bless me and enlarge my territory! Let your hand be with me, and keep me from harm so that I will be free from pain. 1 Chronicles 4:10

Lord, there is no one like you to help the powerless against the mighty. Help us, O Lord our God, for we rely on you, and in your name we have come against this vast army. O Lord, you are our God; do not let man prevail against you. 2 Chronicles 14:11

O our God…we have no power to face this vast army that is attacking us. We do not know what to do, but our eyes are upon you. 2 Chronicles 20:12

O Lord, how many are my foes! How many rise up against me! Many are saying of Me, "God will not deliver him." But you are a shield around me, O Lord; you bestow glory on me and lift up my head… Arise, O Lord! Deliver me, O my God! Psalm 3:1-3,7

Let all who take refuge in you be glad; let them sing for joy. Spread your protection over them, that those who love your name may rejoice in you. For surely, O Lord, you bless the righteous; you surround them with favor as with a shield. Psalm 5:11-12

Keep me safe, O God, for in you I take refuge... Lord you have assigned me my portion and my cup; you have made my lot secure. The boundary lines have fallen for me in pleasant places... Psalm 16:1,5,6

I call on you, O God, for you will answer me; give ear to me and hear my prayer. Show the wonder of your love, you who save by your right hand those who take refuge in you from their foes. Keep me as the apple of your eye; hide me in the shadow of your wings... Psalm 17:6-8

Turn to me and be gracious to me... Guard my life and rescue me; let me not be put to shame, for I take refuge in you. Psalm 25:16,20

In you, O Lord, I have taken refuge; let me never be put to shame; deliver me in your righteousness. Turn your ear to me, come quickly to my rescue; be my rock of refuge, a strong fortress to save me. Since you are my rock and my fortress, for the sake of your name lead me and guide me. Psalm 31:1-3

Do not withhold your mercy from me, O Lord; may your love and truth always protect me... Be pleased, O Lord, to save me; O Lord come quickly to help me... You are my help and my deliverer, O my God, do not delay. Psalm 40:11,13,17

Deliver me from my enemies, O God; protect me from those who rise up against me... O my Strength, I watch for you; you, O God, are my fortress, my loving God... I will sing of your strength, in the morning I will sing of your love; for you are my fortress, my refuge in times of trouble. O my strength, I sing praise to you; you, O God are my fortress, my loving God. Psalm 59:1,9,10,16,17

Hear my cry, O Lord, listen to my prayer. From the ends of the earth I call to you. I call as my heart grows faint; lead me to the rock that is higher than I. For you have been my refuge and a strong tower against the foe. I long to dwell in your tent forever and take refuge in the shelter of your wings. Psalm 61:1-4

In you, O Lord I have taken refuge; let me not be put to shame. Rescue me and deliver me in your righteousness; turn your ear to me and save me. Be my rock of refugee, to which I can always go; give the command to save me, for you are my rock and my fortress. Psalm 71:1-2

Be not far from me, O God; come quickly, O my God, to help me... But as for me I will always have hope; I will praise you more and more. My mouth will tell of your righteousness, of your salvation all day long. Psalm 71:12,14,15

Hear, O Lord, and answer me, for I am poor and needy. Guard my life for I am devoted to you. You are my God, save your servant who trusts in you. Have mercy on me, O Lord, for I call on you all day long. Psalm 86:1-2

O Sovereign Lord, deal well with me for your name's sake; out of the goodness of your love deliver me... Help me. O Lord my God; save me in accordance with your love. Psalm 109:21,26

May your unfailing love come to me, O Lord, your salvation according to your promise... You are my refuge and my shield; I have put my hope in your word. Psalm 119:41,114

Rescue me, O Lord, from evil men; protect me from men of violence, who devise evil plans in their hearts... O Lord, I say, "you are my God." Hear, O Lord, my cry for mercy. O Sovereign Lord, my strong deliverer, who shields my head. Psalm 140:1-2,6-7

I cry to you, O Lord, I say, "you are my refuge, my portion in the land of the living." Listen to my cry, for I am in desperate need... Psalm 142:5-6

Chapter 9

Prayers for Strength and Power

Where do we find the strength and power to live the life God has called us to live and do the things God has given us to do? The answer is, God promises us the strength and power to do everything he has asked of us. The Apostle Paul said, *I can do everything through him who gives me strength* (Philippians 4:13). God makes his strength and power available to us when we ask. In the Bible we find the prayers of people who turned to God for strength and power. Their prayers can be our prayers as we look to God for his strength and power for our lives.

Yours, O Lord, is the greatness and the power and the glory and the majesty and the splendor. For everything in heaven and earth is yours. Yours, O Lord is the kingdom; you are exalted as head over all. Wealth and honor come from you; you are ruler over all things. In your hands are strength and power to exalt and give strength to all. 1 Chronicles 29:11-12

Lord, there is no one to help the powerless against the mighty. Help us, O Lord our God, for we rely on you, and in your name we have come against this vast army. O Lord, you are our God, do not let man prevail against us. 2 Chronicles 14:11

You, O Lord, are a compassionate and gracious God, slow to anger, abounding in love and faithfulness. Turn to me and have mercy on me; grant strength to your servant. Psalm 86:15-16

My soul is weary with sorrow, strengthen me according to your word. Psalm 119:28

O Lord, be gracious to us; we long for you. Be our strength every morning, our salvation in time of distress. Isaiah 33:2

Sovereign Lord, you made the heavens and the earth and the sea, and
everything in them. You spoke by the Holy Spirit through the mouth
of your servant, our father David: "Why do the nations rage and the
people plot in vain? The kings of the earth take their stand and the
rulers gather together against the Lord and against his Anointed One."
…Now, Lord consider their threats and enable your servants to speak
your word with great boldness. Stretch out your hand to heal and
perform miraculous signs and wonders through the name of your holy
servant Jesus." Acts 4:24-26,29-30

I keep asking that the God of our Lord Jesus Christ, the glorious Father,
may give you the Spirit of wisdom and revelation, so that you may
know him better. I pray also that the eyes of your heart may be
enlightened in order that you may know the hope to which he has
called you, the riches of his glorious inheritance in the saints, and his
incomparably great power for us who believe. That power is like the
working of his mighty strength which he exerted in Christ when he
raised him from the dead… Ephesians 1:17-20

For this reason I kneel before the Father, from whom his whole family
in heaven and on earth derives its name. I pray that out of his glorious
riches he may strengthen you with power through his Spirit in your
inner being, so that Christ may dwell in your hearts through faith.
And I pray that you, being rooted and established in love, may have
power, together with all the saints, to grasp how wide and deep is the
love of Christ and to know this love that surpasses knowledge – that
you may be filled to the measure of all the fullness of God. Now to him
who is able to do immeasurably more than all we ask or imagine,
according to his power that is at work within us, to him be glory in
the church and in Christ Jesus throughout all generations, for ever
and ever! Amen. Ephesians 3:14-21

May the Lord make your love increase and overflow for each other
and everyone else, just as our does for you. May he strengthen your
hearts so that you will be blameless and holy in the presence of our

God and Father when our Lord Jesus comes with his holy ones. 1 Thessalonians 3:12-13

May our Lord Jesus Christ himself and God our Father, who loved us and by his grace gave us eternal encouragement and good hope, encourage your hearts and strengthen you in every good deed and word. 2 Thessalonians 2:16-17

Chapter 10

Prayers of Thanksgiving

All that we have, including the very air we breath, comes from the hand of God, yet, many of us, if we are honest, are not very grateful. If God answers a major prayer request we will utter a word of thanks. When we do offer prayers of thanksgiving they are usually for specific things. Even then, the prayers we offer asking for these things are usually more heartfelt than the prayers of thanksgiving. We need to learn to have a heart of gratitude. We need to thank God for all the things he gives us that we never even thought to ask for. In the Bible we find some prayers of thanksgiving that we can use as we learn to be a grateful people.

Save us, O God our Savior; gather us and deliver us from the nations, that we may give thanks to your holy name, that we may glory in your praise. 1 Chronicles 16:35

Praise to you, O Lord, God of our father Israel, from everlasting to everlasting. Yours, O Lord, is the greatness and the power and the glory and the majesty and the splendor. For everything in heaven and earth is yours. Yours, O Lord is the kingdom; you are exalted as head over all. Wealth and honor come from you; you are ruler over all things. In your hands are strength and power to exalt and give strength to all. Now, our God, we give you thanks, and praise your glorious name... Everything comes from you, and we have given you only what comes from your hand. 1 Chronicles 29:10-14

We give thanks to you, O God, we give thanks, for your Name is near; men tell of your wonderful deeds. Psalm 75:1

O Lord, truly I am your servant, the son of your maidservant; you have freed me from my chains. I will sacrifice a thank offering to you and call on the name of the Lord. Psalm 116:16-17

I will give thanks, for you answered me; you have become my salvation... You are my God and I will give you thanks; you are my God and I will exalt you. Psalm 118:21,28

Chapter 11

Prayers of Vindication

All of us have been hurt by others. We have been betrayed by others. Others have gossiped about us. We have been treated unfairly. We have been falsely accused. Others have done us wrong. When these things happen to us, often we want to get even, to pay the other person back. But God has a better plan. The Bible tells us in Romans 12:17,19, *Do not repay anyone evil for evil. Be careful to do what is right in the eyes of everybody... Do not take revenge, my friends but leave room for God's wrath, for it is written: "it is mine to avenge; I will repay," says the Lord.*

People in the Bible were also mistreated and wronged. They were treated unjustly. What did they do? They turned to God for vindication. And that is where we need to turn when we have been hurt by others. We can use the prayers of vindication the Bible in the Bible used to cry out to God for justice.

Hear, O Lord, my righteous plea; listen to my cry. Give ear to my prayer – it does not rise from deceitful from deceitful lips. May my vindication come from you; may your eyes see what is right. Psalm 17:1-2

Vindicate me, O God and plead my cause...rescue me from deceitful and wicked men. You are my God my stronghold... Send forth your light and your truth, them guide me. Psalm 43:1,2,3

Save me, O God, by your name; vindicate me by your might. Hear my prayer, O God; listen to the words of my mouth. Psalm 54:1-2

Rise up, O God, and defend your cause; remember how fools mock you all day long. Do not ignore the clamor of your adversaries, the uproar of your enemies which rises continually. Psalm 74:22-23

O Lord, the God who avenges, O God who avenges shine forth. Rise up, O Judge of the earth; pay back to the proud what they deserve. Psalm 94:1-2

O God, whom I praise, do not remain silent, for wicked and deceitful men have opened their mouths against me; they have spoken against me with lying tongues. With words of hatred they surround me; they attack me without cause. In return for my friendship they accuse me, but I am a man of prayer. Psalm 109:1-4

Chapter 12

Prayers of Worship

For many of us in our western, fast-paced, technological society, worship may be the most difficult area of prayer. We know how to petition God. We know how to approach God on behalf of others. We know how to express our appreciation to God. We may even be able to praise God for what he has done. But when it comes to worshipping God for who and what he is, many of us struggle. The prayers of worship found in the Bible can help us get started. As we use the prayers of worship found in the Bible we will start to get comfortable with worship and we will eventually be able to begin forming our own prayers of worship. God is worthy of our worship and he has given us prayers in his Word to help us give him the worship he deserves. Let us use his Word to worship him.

Who among the gods is like you, O Lord? Who is like you, majestic in holiness, awesome in glory, working wonders? Exodus 15:11

My heart rejoices in the Lord… There is no one holy like the Lord; there is no one besides you; there is no rock like our God… 1 Samuel 2:1,2

How great you are, O Sovereign Lord! There is no one like you and no god but you. 2 Samuel 7:22

O Lord God…there is no God like you in heaven above or earth below, you who keep your covenant of love with your servants who continue wholeheartedly in your way. 1 Kings 8:23

Yours, O Lord, is the greatness and the power and the glory and the majesty and the splendor, for everything in heaven and on earth is yours. Yours, O Lord, is the kingdom; you are exalted as head over all. Wealth and honor come from you; you are the ruler of all things. In your hands are strength and power to exalt and give strength to all. Now, our God, we give you thanks and praise your glorious name. 1 Chronicles 29:11-13

Blessed be your glorious name, and may it be exalted above all blessing and praise. You alone are the Lord. You made the heavens, even the highest heavens, and all their starry host, the earth and all that is on it, the seas and all that is in them. You give life to everything and the multitudes of heaven worship you. Nehemiah 9:5-6

Be exalted, O God, above the heavens, let your glory be over all the earth. Psalm 57:8

O God you are my God, earnestly I seek you; my soul thirsts for you, my body longs for you... I have seen you in the sanctuary and beheld your power and glory. Because your love is better than life, my lips will glorify you. I will praise you as long as I live, and in your name I will lift up my hands. Psalm 63:1-4

How lovely is your dwelling place, O Lord Almighty! My soul yearns, even faints for the courts of the Lord; my heart and my flesh cry out for the living God... Better is one day in your courts than a thousand elsewhere; I would rather be a doorkeeper in the house of my God than dwell in the tents of the wicked. For the Lord is a sun and a shield... O Lord Almighty, blessed is the man who trusts in you. Psalm 84:1,2,10,11,12

Among the gods there is none like you, O Lord; no deeds can compare with yours. All the nations you have made will come and worship before you, O Lord; they will bring glory to your name. For you are great and do marvelous deeds; you alone are God. Psalm 86:8-10

For you, O Lord, are the Most High over all the earth; you are exalted far above all gods. Psalm 97:9

O Lord, you are my God; I will exalt you and praise you're your name, for in perfect faithfulness you have done marvelous things. Isaiah 25:1

Our Father in heaven, hallowed be your name, your kingdom come, your will be done on earth as it is in heaven. Matthew 6:9-10

Holy, holy, holy is the Lord God almighty, who was and is and is to come… You are worthy our Lord and God to receive glory honor and power, for ever and ever! Revelation 4:8,11

To him who sits on the throne and to the Lamb be praise and honor and glory and power, for ever and ever! Revelation 5:13

Praise and glory and wisdom and thanks and honor and power and strength be to our God forever and ever. Amen! Revelation 7:12

Great and marvelous are your deeds, Lord God Almighty. Just and true are your ways, O King of the Ages. Who will not fear you, O Lord, and bring glory to your name? For you alone are holy. All nations will come and worship before you, your righteous acts have been revealed. Revelation 15:3-4